A LOT OF THE WAY
TREES WERE WALKING

A Lot of the Way Trees Were Walking

Poems from the Gospel of Mark

For Roger –
no words or poems
can do justice to my thanks
for your friendship and

CYNTHIA BRIGGS KITTREDGE

our sharing the long and
windy road .
  love and prayers,
        Cynthia

WIPF & STOCK · Eugene, Oregon

A LOT OF THE WAY TREES WERE WALKING
Poems from the Gospel of Mark

Wipf & Stock
An Imprint of Wipf and Stock Publishers
199 W. 8th Ave., Suite 3
Eugene, OR 97401

www.wipfandstock.com

ISBN 13: 978-1-4982-0050-9

Manufactured in the USA.

I dedicate this book in gratitude to the students
at Seminary of the Southwest with whom I have read, interpreted, and
proclaimed Holy Scripture in classroom, in chapel, and in community.

"And the man looked up and said, "I can see people, but they look like trees, walking."

–MARK 8:24

Contents

Contents

Contents

Preface

"…and he was with the wild beasts." −Mark 1:13

That fragment of a line from the gospel of Mark provokes and intrigues me. It epitomizes Mark's laconic and austere style. "With"? How "with"? Are these beasts friendly or fierce? Are we to imagine Eden or enmity? Other gospels supply dialogue and overlook the animals, but Mark has that empty desert with Jesus, Satan, and those unidentified beasts. The lack of explanation refuses answers, but invites inquiry and wonder.

For many years I have read the gospel of Mark with classes of students and explored the world of the text from its first word to its final conjunction. I have insisted that we stick with Mark only, seek to recognize Mark's own logic, and to live in that symbolic world. Working through the narrative, year after year, I have only grown more entranced by the repetition, the limited vocabulary of elemental words: "ground," "seed," "way," and the insoluble parables and paradoxes. In the course, Biblical Interpretation for Preaching, students learn to read carefully, to use scholarship judiciously, to see each episode in the context of the whole narrative and then preach a sermon.

I wrote these poems in the early mornings during one semester of the course where we read Mark. I read the gospel from the beginning; I tackled whatever puzzle or detail seized me; and I set out to work it through or play it out with a poem. I stayed as long as I wanted in a place in the gospel, moved on when I wished, and I didn't try to cover everything. For many days I thought I would never move beyond "beginning." I did not go back to poems from earlier days. I kept reading and writing forward until the day I reached the end of Mark.

The experience of writing this cycle of poems was unlike Biblical Interpretation for Preaching in many ways. Different because I didn't follow the rules of the discipline of biblical studies: I asked questions the text wasn't answering. I read from the point of view of animals. I thought about plants. I mixed up the gender of characters. I read myself into the text. I thought about the resonances of English words in translation as well as the Greek vocabulary. My experimenting was fueled by inexhaustible fascination with the gospel and supported by appreciation for the Markan scholars who had taught me so much about this text. Unlike biblical interpretation for preaching, there was no goal to "translate" a passage into spiritual learning or a moral lesson. There was no pressure to find relevance. In this way my exploring of scripture was, as my colleague Ellen Bradshaw Aitken describes, "immersive" rather than "instrumental."[1]

At the same time this project originated in my teaching. In teaching scripture at a seminary I have ventured outside the rationalism of the discipline. I have encouraged immersion and attention in addition to and sometimes instead of, analysis and solution. In an early assignment preaching students have performed passages from Mark. In their performances they do not say what a parable or an account of a deed of power "means" with other words, but they interpret through their telling of the text in the text's own words. Many of these tellings are as powerful as any sermon. In other courses I have given a final assignment to interpret a passage from the scripture we were studying using a medium other than discursive prose. Students have written songs and poems. They have used watercolor, made collages from found objects, cooked meals, thrown and fired pots. The exercise exhibits that every interpretation is a re-making. We were often amazed how we would have a fresh encounter with the scripture through these projects. For many years I appreciated and affirmed these things they made without realizing how I hungered to make myself. So I returned to pleasures of my childhood. I began again to play with color and materials. I began again to write poems. Then one autumn I made this poem cycle "from" the gospel of Mark.

---

1. Ellen Bradshaw Aitken, presentation at Anglican Association of Biblical Scholars Annual Meeting, Baltimore, MD 2013. Aitken uses the term "saturated" for "immersive" in "Relentless Intimacy: The Peculiar Labor of an Anglican Biblical Scholar," *Anglican Theological Review* 93/4 (2011) 563–580.

Preface

These poems reflect my engagement with the gospel of Mark. The book is an account of my genuine experience of a stunningly beautiful, cruel, and hopeful text. It represents a "reading" of the text, a re-making, but one that is not comprehensive, final, or universal.

I think that it is difficult to have a genuine experience of reading scripture – to be open, to suspend disbelief, to enter it wholeheartedly, and to discover. All the "shoulds" around the Bible create obstacles to genuine experience. There are centuries of commentary telling us what it means. It has to be serious. It has to be profound. I have to like it. It should make me feel good and holy. Everyone else understands it, but me. All these expectations inhibit attentive, immersive reading and deny distracted twenty-first century people the ability to be curious and possibility of joy and wonder incited by these texts.

I hope that these poems might encourage your own entry into the gospel of Mark and instigate your own conversation. They may serve as a means of immersion and attention.

Next to its mystery, the other striking feature of the gospel is the courage of its heroes – those who dig through the roof on behalf of their friend, the one who chases, and the one who throws off the cloak. It might be that these poems make you bold. To read. To make. To have faith.

Austin, Texas June 2014

Acknowledgments

I am grateful to those who read these poems and encouraged me to share them. I thank the Anglican Association of Biblical Scholars for inviting me to read and speak about the project at their annual dinner in 2013, and Ellen Jockusch, Jane Patterson, Claire Miller Colombo, Ruthanna Hooke, Jared Houze, and Jim Crosby for reading the manuscript in its early stages. I thank Greg Garrett for his experience and advice. I thank Peter Cunningham and Ara Fitzgerald for both listening and hearing. I thank Peter also for his photograph on the cover. Finally, I thank Elizabeth Struthers Malbon who helped to shape this collection by her close reading and perceptive editorial suggestions.

Begin

Mark 1:1–15

What Shall I Cry?

Way before I reached that turning point
of not knowing what to cry
I had to ask for years and years,
shall I?

Throw myself off
Fall a shooting star
streaked naked light
flesh a phrase
in the night, visible,
back to dark.

Can I?
Dare with trembling ink
to spill to mark to soil
blank white wilderness
erase the possibility
for anything else to grow
there but that. But you.
Indelible.

Open my lips make me a mouth
inhale air prepare
wait at the edge
of silence
darkness
whiteness
to

Jordan

There's a mass confessing going on
the river is crowded and cold.
How deep do we need
to dive
how dark?

Too soon off stage
out of sight
the Ripper, the Render, the Splitter
comes to divide.

Prophecy

Look it up
Send a text
Track the waste
Make it straight.

In Folsom Prison
the train whines
he hangs his head
and cries.

Prophet

He preached with water.
Wash and Brush.

He looked the part.
Acquainted with bees.

Mightier even.
Just you wait.

Desert

Spirit light as pigeon feather
deceives us when she comes
on greeting cards cross-stitched on cushions

Heaving up she catapults
into the wild far away
for a session of testing
the one she loves.

Abstract

unrealing
revealing
unveiling

unvealing
reveiling
rerealing

Tear

veil rending
un winding
re mending

Apocalypse

Look up into the gash in the splitten sky
it widens and brightens to reveal
flocks of crippled sheep, men with withered arms
shattered legs, women bleeding, children siezing,
pallets stacked like packing crates.
Keep your seat, wait and watch unreal
wind blowing, fevers leaving foreheads,
limbs grown back sanity restored
dead children waking up
and just before the heavens mend,
hills covered with bread.

Follow

Mark 1:16–8:21

Because

For they were brothers
For they were fishers
For they were sons
For he said Follow.

Entries

Andrew, brother of Simon
Galilee, Sea of
James, brother of John
John, brother of James
Simon, brother of Andrew
Zebedee, father

See also, Peter.

In Waiting

The angels departed their posts
    in the heavenly court
to hover in the prickly pear
and wait.

Awatch for stinging, slashing things,
they are available
to sweep in and lift up
    if necessary
the child in their charge.

Prone, laid out in the parlor
    almost ash
unable to protect or feed or carry
anyone in her arms,
mother was going to be gone
    before the story began.

She reached out her hand, held on
and she was lifted up
born up on the back of the sea
    raised high above the other winds.
She came back to us from the fire
took her place at our table
to attend and wait.

Fierce Industry

One kept watch, sought an opening.
She got the mallet
he brought the awl
she rigged the litter, truss, and shackle.
Up they scrambled,
down they tunneled,
lowered the pallet into the hall.
Jesus looked up, ceiling torn open,
down came the man suspended,
descending like a holy bird.
He didn't see the cunning, versatile friends,
but their love looked just like faith.

Party

The wine was new.
Whores and crooks were all invited.
They helped themselves to seconds and thirds.
When the band struck up, he asked her,
"Would you consider this slow?"
Arms around, brow to brow
they danced like there was no tomorrow.

Outlaw

Nobody's where they belong.
Not in their own skin.
Not in their right mind.
Not at home with their mother and sibs
but out worrying the neighbors.

If you're not at home
someone else could be eating off your table
sitting in your chair
sleeping in your bed.

Not a little towhead
but a Bad Man
Burgler
Lord of the Flies.

Recruit reinforcements, enlist allies
a gang to gag and duct tape
him tightly to a chair.

Look into the parable
join in the hills watch
from a distance
splitting shattering falling
the end of his house.

Where to Look

What's another word for kingdom?
Reign, rule, era, aeon, epoch,
term, regime, sphere,
administration,
galaxy of God.

You can look up to the heaven and hope it opens
or lower your gaze to the soil
see what the seed is doing,
hungry birds and scorching sun—
rocks.
Somewhere she beats the odds
germinates—
the galaxy is born.

Weather

Does it ever rain in the Bible on an ordinary day?
When no resolution to destroy the world is underway
but only a gentle drizzle and reverberating gray
causes words to shimmer
we resolve to stay.

Clarification

Not all parables are short and sweet.
Some are long and mean.
Parables separate keep
out the chaff make
eyes blind
ears shut
define who's in
and who's
not.

Animals

Animals in Mark starting with the wild beasts who wait on him also
moving on to the fowls of the air who devour the seed
but in between there are some more animals—yes, the bees
and the locusts and the camels,
more about wildness, uncultivated nourishment
grace like grits that just comes.
Back to the raptors—
A raptor went out to rapt.
The seed that eluded their beaks
somehow got buried not along the way
but in some purposeful place where the dirt was dark.
It bloomed and grew tall and cast shade,
an oasis for the predators to rest.

Wisdom

Earth and heaven
earth is brown and sky is blue
earth is solid and heaven is air.
Look up into the torn open heaven
see what should be, what is to be, what really is.
Weird stuff that is brilliant, lampstands,
crowns cast on a glassy sea
wheels within wheels
in need of translation.
Or just keep walking on the ground
check out the blooming weeds
mud puddles drying from puddle to mud
sparrows being sparrows
in every nation
what really is.

Amos Niven Wilder

I remember he was thin just right a bit gaunt
spare like the typeface looks on the page
letters stricken by ribbon.
A name given not made
born.
American in the beautiful romantic way
prophet of Israel haunting
and the desert written into you.
If there were an actual era
when poets could write about the gospels
he summoned it up
made me long to go there.
Perhaps he belonged in the world
because of his name
or he lived into the name he was named.
He wrote about Mark, another sharp one,
parables of disappointment
and fertility
blessing.

Intercalation

Neither has a name
one dies
one bleeds
each at the point of no returning.

The old one interrupts
the multitude
the master
occupied with his errand of mercy.

Dangerously grazing
his fringes
innermost parts sort and fold relay
that she will live.

Brush upon unguarded flank
reverses
blood and power
causes both to tremble.

The dead one sleeps
deeply no hurry
for her to rise
hungry.

Stone

Once I stumbled, stumbled so as to fall.
I discovered that falling is the most common cause of emergency room
    visits.
People fall all the time, off chairs, on sidewalks, changing lightbulbs.
Crashing is what it is really—colliding to earth
face planting, wrist twisting, teeth shattering.
Stumbling can mean wreckage or a near miss.

When sisters stumble, stumble and wonder
at wisdom and power, demons ravished and running, girls rising from
    the dead,
law enforcement engaged in counter terrorism,
they might catch themselves, get their footing beneath them,
recover. Or along with the stars and the temple and the old world
    order
they might be ruined.

Herod Says

This would be him reheaded
raising hell.
Why won't they stay in their tombs
even when shackled with chains?
Why don't they surrender
bleeding, bleeding, bleeding?
Even pretty girl corpses
get up
to eat another day.
He was sleeping the big sleep.
There is going to be more trouble.

Antonym

What's the opposite of holy?
In my child opposed to holy
is cutting herself and gagging,
pulling out her hair
scarring and piercing
the smooth and the whole.

I shout out for holy
call by name the one who owns her claws
possesses her maw.
I cry for holy to contend and destroy
mighty, decisive.
Buy her back for herself.

Repartee

Dirty Sprite
Afflicting
Her Child.
She begged.
He said No.
My Child.
Not Dog.
She said Yes.
My Child
Too.
She won.
Starve a cold
Feed a demon
Gone Fiend.
My Child.

Feast of Crumbs

The whole litter convened
beneath the feast
scrambled, tumbled warm fur shining
not since they were weaned
have they been filled
let in from the raw back yard
spilled bread
red as meat
take and eat
then sleep the sleep of the healed.

See

Mark 8:22–10:52

Downside

All was black
he could stay in
town.
When he saw men like
trees
walking
he was our peer
he had lots of company
all those other
trees.
When all was clear
he could never
go
back.

Resolution

Once you get the trees resolved
             into people
then you have to sort out
             what name applies
to this holy man who opens
             eyes
unstops ears
             wrestles
demons to the ground.

So you get him pegged.

See clearly hear
     well
make sense
     right mind now.

Now dissolve order give
             away
what you thought you got
             misplace
what you thought
             you found
completely change your
             attitude
clarity requires
             you to forfeit.

I am longing for the forest.

Clarity

When the trees were walking
the shadows in motion limpid green and blonde
jostled and stilled.

The play of dark patches
made you recognize the sun
your sisters' faces, the children.

Today it's all glare
glistening brilliant bleach
and ultimatum: die, deny
or be ashamed.

Certain

Fear shuts mouths
Fear stops tongues
makes you dumb as a lamb
silent as sea.

Or if it doesn't succeed
in keeping you quiet
it causes you to
sound stupid.

Send them away.
We have no bread.
A ghost!

We have arrived.
Let us set up
three tents for you here
in the dazzling shade.

Prediction

they will
mock
spit
flog
kill

he will
be rejected
be betrayed
suffer
die

rise
go ahead
meet
you

Thrown

I was the most in control little girl.
My oxfords were laced and tied neatly.
I studied
I filled in the ovals darkly
with a number two pencil.

At night I knew differently
falling usually a long way and not
knowing where
or who I had become
self shaking mouth agaping
help, help, help, wanting to call
get somebody to come
hold me make it stop
another wave I was taken over
inside and racked within
set to rattling
silent screaming.

I didn't ask myself
which is me or why
or who took me and threw me
down.

What I believed was
my mother and my father
picking me up holding me
assuring me
that it was morning.

Limit

We could follow instructions
about how to cook for a crowd
to count heads and multiply
measure so it would come out right
four thousand servings.
We could obey directions for
the number of miles on the road to go
where to ford the sea
how steep the hill will be
and arrive at the city in time for the feast.

We could put the teaching
in order and arrange the sequence
why Elijah comes first
how two become one
whom to love most and before all.

Why can't we conjure bread?
Why can't we cast it out?
Why aren't they following us?

Complaints get riddles and queries
elicit queer suggestions:
see this baby and be full of wonder
better to be maimed and half blind
drink this terrible cup.

Escape

The text has been on that page for a very long time.
Might as well have been forever.
Right there between the covers
available mysteries.

My words I snatch from the early morning air.
If I'm lucky.
Each short line shallowly engraved
taking a stab at what I might know.

Yesterday it was trying to penetrate
the logic of instruction that mystifies.
The master predicts, he proverbs, determined it seems
to flummox.

First I use the liquid ink sliding on paper
then mind transmits to lighted screen
the closest marks I can muster
to tangle with the teacher and the teaching.

Then it was done. It has to be.
When time runs out and day begins.
Do you want to save the changes you made to "ALotofTheWayTrees.
 docx"?
I declined. Right pointer finger touched, Don't Save.

Gone. I cannot retrieve it from the Trash
where it isn't. Or from AutoSave
which was not On. What were the words I had spotted and trapped
in Microsoft Word for Mac? What track did they make?

Road

I couldn't see until I was naked.
When I could see I became naked.

I took off my clothes and followed.

Unbind me, unbind me. Take me with you.

Garment

His sister was the bleeding one who sought him in the mob,
ducked among the maimed and lame,
outskirted the twelve with names
to snatch the power from the cloak he wore.

He shouted for mercy, for mercy so loudly he was finally heard,
you've got a chance they said,
seize it and get up. He dropped his wrap for he was
asked a question to be answered naked.

Shadow

I've followed through the countryside
along the roads and sea—
I've seen the blind eyes open wide
the shackled man made free.

I've listened with my unstopped ears
heard proverbs queer and stark
fear despite the power unleashed
the gospel be so dark.

The roadside is scattered with stones
and seared with scorching sun
the human one will be alone
betrayed forsaken done.

I search to see a glimpse of light
of company and kin
Recall now how the girl rose bright
and ate the meal within.

When the lonely daughter dying
pursued and grabbed his robe
she becomes in desperate trying
a heroine of hope.

Does light and darkness alternate,
day follows after night?
Or do life and death comingle—
one crucible of might?

Enter

Mark 11:1–12:44

Enter

Waving fronds of acacia, laying down a carpet of pine,
the grateful and hopeful carry cypress boughs, greet with laurel limbs,
usher in with emerald willow sprays. Along the winding road
stretch broadleaf branches, strew wild shoots of tamarisk, pistacia
weave a sweet green way.

Acclaim

Hooray, Hooray
Hurrah, Hurrah
Hosanna

Hurry, Hurry
Help, Help
Hosanna

Save Us
Save Us
Save Us

Hosanna

Ready

There have been too few animals since
the desert.
Only some hapless sheep, a herd
of pigs possessed.
In medias res there happens
a colt tied up so you don't have to chase it
just there
never ridden. Why? Too young, just back from the country
tethered, available
to play the role of a lifetime.

Sunday

The fronds of palm were soft
underfoot
the sap where they were cut
fragrant.

Pray

Holy One, please take this mountain,
lift it up and throw it into the sea.
While you're at it, make the leaves grow back
     and the fruit come.
Build up the walls within the ruins, and put
away my crime.

Leaves

Nothing but leaves.
We are grateful
for leaves considering
we have come all this way
as pilgrims.
They are green and fragile
like our faith.

Curse

Sour Grapes
Damn You
No Grow
You Rob
So Go
To Hell

Parable

That was one bloody estate.
Again and again he sent envoys
to collect
and they never came back.
If you ask me he should have shut the whole thing down
way sooner.

Whole Life

Here were the riddles:
the one headed coin,
the overtired widow,
the love scribe
who was very close,
and the Lord joke.
Then the punch line.
All is more.

Watch

Mark 13:1–37

Discourse

They read flat and in sequence and we teach
them to read in multiple
dimensions.
A dialogue set in the past is
about the future
that wasn't really future then
but already past
even though described as coming.
The whole of it is past now—
the stones scattered,
the leaders astray,
endless wars.
The days cut short have gone on
it seems like forever,
when we think no suffering has ever been so severe
and prolonged and cruel
that the time has finally come.
Still we endure, we stay awake and wonder
how the fig grows green again
and how the sun rises brilliant, burns and sets, then
the moon takes her place.
Both keep
their steady shining thrones.

Regret

The House fell down we already know it did,
after it was mucked up, desecrated beyond imagining.
It was all undone by the thundering horses and riders
not one stone upon stone, neither shingle on shingle,
no longer line upon line
any precept upon precept.
By then there was no longer a whisper
of prayer there
any breath at all.
What I miss, what I lament, grieve without letup
and will not stop or be at rest
while I have life
are the beaches of sand, the snow whitening the mountains
the flowers blooming in the desert.

Don't

If you stay awake through all the tribulations, your own troubles,
the turmoil of your people and of all the nations,
then you will learn as from the fig tree and all the other parables
that there isn't going to be any one definitive sign.
You might think it will be the destruction of east Asian islands
so many dead fishermen
and the disgorging of sea monsters that no one has ever seen.
Or the drowning of New Orleans its music and cuisine
how many black people washed up and how poor
how old hooked up to IV's and ventilators
all yanked out by the water, stranded on roofs
rotted everything shooting stealing scrambling to escape.
You might mistake for the last day
the down thundering Towers, the atomized
paper and flesh, concrete, transfigured into a cloud that darkened the
      sun,
descended and silenced the islands, the mainland
the mighty and the humble.
Or for the terminal, the Federal Building exploded
and leveled
out on the plains under the wide sky
there's a new park now.
These are not final. They will preach
that you and your fathers have sinned. They will create out of the dust
new adversaries to oppose and to hate
with hottest hate. Do not go after them.
The earth cracks open and people fall within the smashing rocks.
The seas burst their bounds and wash the cities away.
Huge oaks will be afflicted with blight. Great trees will fall by
      themselves
and crush what is underneath.
You will suffer as humans do, your child quaking, seizing,
your husband gone mad, breaking rocks,
your mother burning up.

Your own hand will wither and your eyesight fade
to black.
No corporate cataclysm will stop life
being full of losing. Endure on tenterhooks
hold the nursing child with the hand you have left
scent in the damp darkness the seed in the soil
clinging to the scattered stones.
During the wakeful night, hear
the sound of it sprouting.

Break

Mark 14:1–15:20

How

If you want to follow
you have to risk
humiliation
embarrassment
failure.
You have to be prepared
to lose everything
and then lose it.
The widow gave her coins
the anointer her perfume
every last bit
of both.
You have to chase
like the bleeder
yell
like the beggar.
You have to stay alive
when you want to
sleep
You have to stay awake
when you want to
die.
They show you
how.

Forever

Begin at the end with the punch line when she is not just defended but praised to the stars,
where it is declared that what she did
will be remembered not by being engraved on a stone
in some dusty town. (Here she lies. See her name at the head.)
But it will be told everywhere in the whole world—Tyre and Sidon
and Syrophoenecia, the Decapolis, Alexandria, Rome, Spain,
from Jerusalem, in Judea and Samaria, and to the ends of the earth.
They will build cathedrals dedicated to her and compose oratorios
and she will never be far from our minds because there will be major
    feasts in her honor.
Along with bread and wine and water, perfume will be an essential
    element
the stuff of our faith.
Fragrant and smooth, inestimable, it will always mean
that the one who will save will lose, and the one who will die will live.
As omnipresent as the cross, the alabaster box
will be her sign, the perfect jar
that must be shattered.

No

What she has done, her beautiful deed
will never be told.
Not in Tyre or Sidon, Paris, France,
New York, or Rome.

She will be misunderstood
her sacrifice called seduction
her prophecy rejected
her knowledge erased.

Unremarked, unremembered
she will be found
in the negative space
wherever there is silence.

Table

Tables are where people squabble
about who is the greatest
where they criticize the one
who really is.
Tables are where the lepers
whores and tax collectors
eat from the same bowl
fingers greasy.
At tables perfume
is wasted. Wine is poured
out. Bread is given away.

Run

Havoc.
Sheep are spooked.
They run for cover.
Panic.

Rat.
You cannot hide.
You are not safe.
Flee.

Deny.
No one to trust.
Shepherd stricken.
Desert.

Place

They failed to stay awake.
The hour didn't pass.
The cup didn't go.
Trial came.

The only yes
what you will.

Asleep

Peter, James, and John slept
stubbornly
three times in succession
waking only long enough
to fail again.
Lucky for them
not to see
fury, grief, fear
crying in the dirt.

Metal

Back in the country when no one was home
they tried to lay family hands on him. Under their roof
he would remain—not out provoking the attention of elders.

This episode features machinery, simple tools,
that made civilization possible, not the spoon or potters wheel,
wrought swords and clubs, noisy and terrifying in the night.

Clanging, jangling, clanking metal upon metal,
crowd now is hostile and armed, all the authorities with their various
    titles
pressed in. How can you say, who touched me?

Overtaken and outnumbered, identified,
the handover accomplished with only minor incident
one severed ear and a fleet young man.

The pretense of testimony, evidence, the logic
of the courtroom, the doctrinal interrogation
all halted by silence and the promise of more clouds.

Due process degenerates into tantrum of tearing,
sputtering, freakout, outrage, fury. Spit, blindfold, strike, accuse.
Then the guards beat him like guards will do.

Shackles and chains in Gerasene could not restrain
Legion. Cuffs, leg irons, and belly chains, bind tight
and make him safe to hand over again.

Both

It sounds logical but it's not historically
realistic at all.
Psychologically it appears to be totally
realistic.
Mythologically, theologically, fatalistically
also yes.

Charcoal

There is a parallel universe
where fires warm
roosters crow
and people are people.

Routine

Then the soldier mocked and tortured him
as soldiers will do.
They used a cruel crown and a phony scepter.
They pulled the purple cloak over his head
and called in the dogs.

Die

Mark 15:21–47

Fathers

Not all fathers are disappointing, or divine, or absent.
Simon, for instance, whose sons Alexander and Rufus,
are part of his name, undetachable.
Zebedee, remember, was patient when he was stranded by James and
    John.
Jairus pleaded for his daughter to be made well and live,
the girl who bore his name.
The nameless father of the nameless boy, watched the demon
sieze him, throw him to the ground, cast him into the water and into
    the fire
over and over again,
cried out in prayer: "I have faith, help my faithlessness."
They did not abandon. They did not forsake.

Man on a Stick

Man on a stick
secured.
Set upon
compassed about
by a pack of snarling curs.
Their razor terrier teeth snap
bark muzzles snort
released to gorge
feeding frenzy.

No malice
no mockery
within their
animal cortex
instinct alone
gore
lick blood.

Unicorn

If humans had horns, bone in the front of their heads
one or even better two
like the rhinoceros
who has one enormous one for whom he is named
plus one for back up,
they could shake and threaten with them
knock over, spear and pierce
clobber and club
they could butt and bully
strike knock out
disembowel.
If animals had the capacity
for irony or the ability
to shame
they could taunt and sarcastically
inquire why
the mighty one
has no defense.

Dark

Darkness descends to the ground here at our feet
in the dirt at the foot of the dead tree
without roots, bereft of leaves.
Black lack of any relief careens and covers
the regions beyond the city, the Hosanna road,
Jericho, Jordan, Tyre and Sidon.
Thick night spins the cloak woven of heavy
horsehair from exhausted, wasted beasts
and casts it over the seven seas
to shut its million glittering eyes.
Midday midnight
the biological clock of the world
breaks. In the smothering covering
ink you can suddenly see.

Translate

"Eloi Eloi Lama Sabachthani?"
Does it need translation?
Everyone who prays knows that Aramaic
protest, that primal timeless
cry, anyone anyway who has ever
read the story or witnessed even
from a distance
dying, not just life ending
but dying without solace
companionless, terrified.
Rattle racking magnified in the chambers
closing, you have heard that
or you have made that sentence in your own gullet
and know what it means.

Untitled 1

darkness is swallowing up the boy
where is the wind

within it is in the inner dark
it bellows

forth and floats away
with the slightest of wings

Untitled 2

It tore a hole so open
you could walk right through it
never mind peaking in or having to fear
you would be booted out
for even getting too near.

Untitled 3

Announced at the water, my child
pronounced on the mountain, my child
admitted at the Skull place,
for sure the child is dead.

Far

They waited on him from far off
by watching
their eyes glowed
Wolf mothers
alert

Offering

The angels didn't feed the hungering one,
rather they distracted the adversary by flashing
their bright feet
drawing light arcs in the sky.

The multitude groaned for food
and from their woven bags covered with scarlet birds
they offered
loaves and minor fish.

They kept him now also by looking
and seeing, beholding the place
he was laid, so they could remember
and return to minister again.

Sure

Crucified, dead, and buried
Synonymous parallelism, redundancy, or pleonasm
because you are either alive
or not.
On the other hand, when you are so alive that your aliveness
tames the sea and makes bread cover the hills
and makes the world over again, makes the crazy sane
the wounded whole and brings the dying to life,
then your deadness must be made
absolutely certain.
Your final howl.
Testimony by soldier one.
Witness of the women,
especially two mothers and the Magdalene.
Check by Pilate.
Corroboration by soldier two.
Confirmation by Joseph
with his own hands on the flesh
shoulder on the boulder—
the case is watertight—
the women see him
closing the opening
ending the story.

Go

Mark 16:1–8

Promise

I will go before you to Galilee.
Who remembers that promise,
buried back there under the betraying and the deserting?
No one really pays attention—at least
they don't say anything, like
What do you mean?
Why Galilee?
That country will be beautiful like Kansas looks
after you've been to Oz,
when you have seen everything go
to complete hell in Jerusalem.
More splendid than descending clouds
more lovely than fine temple stones
will be the sandy seaside
budding sycamores
of Galilee.

Finish

It is a difficult story to end
when the end is not an end
but a closing that opens
a big door where the big stopper
used to be jammed in
and the something is really
nothing or rather
the nothing that is not there
is what is the something
that even though you didn't know it
can not name it still
is the it the I the living
you have been
wanting

What

Just like he said.
Did he tell that it would be stormy and angels
would hover in a huge noisy host
getting ready to sweep us up
into the firmament where we would shine
as the stars?
Did he say that we would reign with him
after the strong man's house
collapsed?
Did he promise that he would usher us in
seat us next to the golden throne
to drink wine new?
What do you remember?
What do you expect?

What (cont'd)

Remember what you remember
and you will know for what you hope.

Full

That empty space cries to be filled
with pictures of what is really good—
the hearth where she baked the bread
warm and fragrant
and she fed us when she returned from the fire.
The puppies slept under the table.
Our friend who walked out of the torn up house
under his own steam
with his bed under his arm.
Write in the blank spaces the learning
that every day is a day to make
things over again.
all food is clean
all flesh is holy.

See

That hole in the rock
was their mountain of transfiguration
where they were stunned and
stricken with knowledge.
That gaping opening
was the dazzling darkness
teeming, roiling
pregnant with worlds.
It drew them in to see
and rendered them
wordless.

Know

The frustrated conjunction
joins
with nothing
it dangles
into space
a life line
to catch hold of
or simply
to let
loose
into the abyss
of ecstasy

Easter

Maybe the last word will be ending
like the first one was beginning.
Perhaps it should be over
with the dawn
flight.
Or it should conclude
with shuddering silence
as it began with the writing
and the solitary voice.
We have not traveled a circuit
back but followed
a long and winding road
of losing and finding
saving and tossing out
lying down and getting up
sleeping and waking
dying and rising.
A lot of the way
trees were walking
we were ignorant
unmeaning.
So much hurt
how much delight
always it came near
we were not far
and now we are here
the last word is glory.